TT
970
468
1992

28 STYLES

for Student Practice, Second Edition with Basic Cutting and Styling Guides

Kenneth Young

Milady Publishing Company
(A Division of Delmar Publishers, Inc.)
3 Columbia Circle, Box 15015
Albany, NY 12212-5015

EDITOR: Catherine Frangie

ILLUSTRATOR: Robert Richards

PRODUCTION: John Mickelbank

COVER DESIGN: John Fornieri

© Copyright 1992
Milady Publishing Company
(A Division of Delmar Publishers Inc.)
ISBN 1-56253-070-4

**Library of Congress Cataloging-in-Publication
Data**

Young, Kenneth, 1952–
    28 styles for student practice with basic cutting
and styling guides / Kenneth Young.—2nd ed.
      p.   cm.
      ISBN 1-56253-070-4 $7.50

Printed in the United States of America

Delmar Publishers' Online Services
To access Delmar on the World Wide Web, point your browser to:
http://www.delmar.com/delmar.html
To access through Gopher: gopher://gopher.delmar.com
(Delmar Online is part of "thomson.com", an Internet site with information on
more than 30 publishers of the International Thomson Publishing organization.)
For information on our products and services:
email: info@delmar.com
or call 800-347-7707

Directions for Use of This Book

This manual was created in order to help you, the student, develop your manual skills in haircutting and hairstyling in preparation for your eventual licensing examination.

Since you begin with a mannequin having long hair, the styles progress from long to shorter hair and require increasing degrees of manual dexterity. For this reason, it is best that you practice every style in the order in which it appears in this book.

Each style guide first offers CUTTING TECHNIQUES to assist you in cutting your mannequin's hair. Refer to the illustration to determine the exact length required for each area of the head, and to the list of terminology for any haircutting terms that may be unfamiliar to you.

The DESIGN TECHNIQUE offer both illustrated setting patterns and written directions for any techniques being introduced or especially important in executing the style. Follow the styling key to determine whether rollers, brushes or curling irons will best achieve the finished style.

The section on STYLING TECHNIQUE offers you hints that will make completion of the style easier and the finished look more professional. Refer to the illustrations in order to compare your developing style to the finished look desired.

The last two pages of this book contain a scoring guide for your instructor's evaluation of your performance of the styling techniques for each design. Practice each set until your instructor indicates that you are ready to progress to the next style, having demonstrated salon-level competency. After completing this book, you will be prepared for advanced styling techniques, having mastered the basic techniques of cutting and styling.

IMPLEMENTS KEY

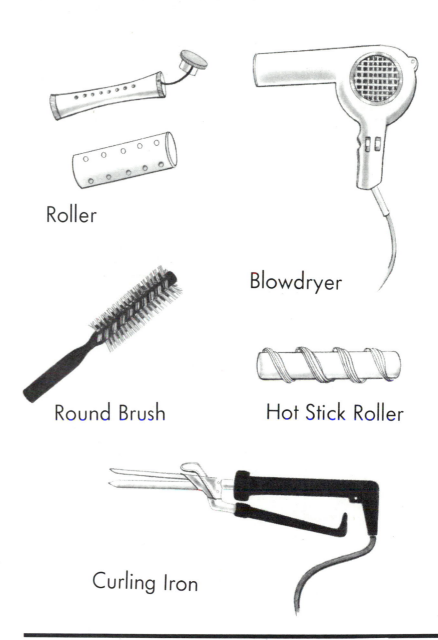

Roller

Blowdryer

Round Brush

Hot Stick Roller

Curling Iron

ROLLER BASE KEY

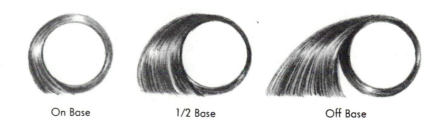

On Base   1/2 Base   Off Base

1

1

Cutting Technique

This is a long reverse elevation haircut. Exterior length is 4½ inches in the front at the bang to 6 inches in the nape. All the hair is pulled straight up and cut to a horizontal plane on top. This will create layers and movement without removing the hanging length. Use a 4 inch guide at top to establish interior length.

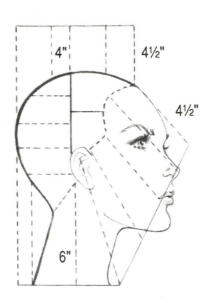

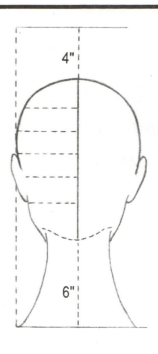

1. On Base
2. 1/2 Base
3. Off Base

Design Technique

Hair is set on rollers in opposing directions. This will create the explosion of curls throughout the head. Hair should wrap around the roller at least 2½ times to curl. On naturally wavy hair, or hair permed on large rods, use the scrunch method of styling. Using the palm of your hand, rub hair in a circular motion, and dry the hair at the same time by directing blow dryer at your hand.

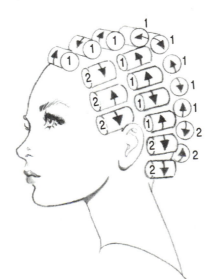

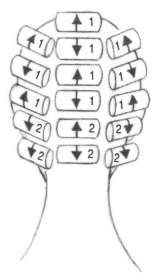

Styling Technique

To style, wet set lightly and brush or comb through each curl. Then using finger tips, tousle the hair to create a soft look. To develop more height and fullness, lightly backcomb hair up to 2 inches from ends. Then using fingers, tousle ends again for a casual look.

Style

Cutting Technique

Cut the guide 6 inches in length from the hairline in the nape. Hair will be parted horizontally, matched to the guide and cut. Do not elevate the hair when cutting. Be sure to stay parallel with the floor. Blend the sides into the back using the length in back as a guide. Be sure to keep the head straight when cutting. If the head moves, the lengths will vary. For detail, create a triangular section from the center of the recession to the top of the crown. Proceed to cut this area to a length of 5 inches holding the hair straight up.

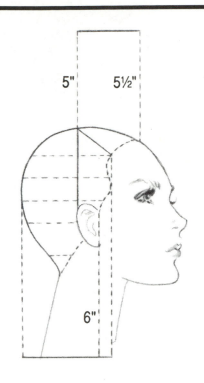
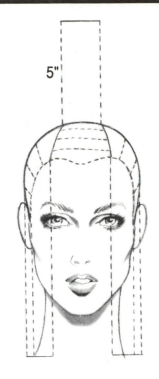

1. On Base
2. 1/2 Base
3. Off Base

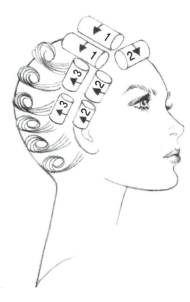

Design Technique

Set rollers first. Top is set in a half bang by directing the rollers diagonally back from the face on the left side. This will leave a triangular section over the right eye. Direct a roller in this section towards the eye. Fill in the rest of the top with rollers directed straight back. The sides will be set diagonally up and back on rollers. Split the back into two sections vertically down the center. On the right, make a vertical row of clockwise pincurls with stems directed diagonally up. On the left, the pincurls will be counterclockwise. This row will overlap the previous row of curls.

Note: The pincurls should be large with a center diameter of 1½ inches.

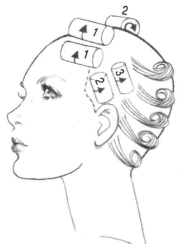
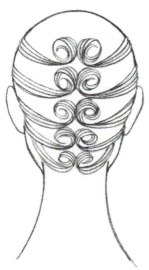

Styling Technique

Brush the hair to soften the set. Then brush all the hair from the right side to the left. Leave the top section out. Using bobbie pins, secure a vertical line off center to the left. Direct the hair back over the center from left to right. Using your left hand, twist the hair counterclockwise working up towards the ends. Use your right hand to tuck and smooth the fold. Secure with bobbie or hair pins. Backcomb the top for height, then comb in waves. Using your fingers, pull down the bang over the right eye.

Note: The french twist can be used on a variety of lengths of hair. Experiment with a variety of styles in the bang area. Use bang styles from other sets in this book.

Style

3

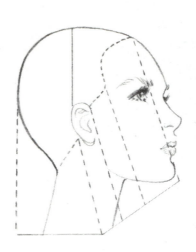

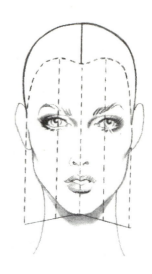

Cutting Technique

Cut a low elevation parallel to the ground. Keep head in a straight forward position as this will create a slight graduation. Front should be angled from behind the ear to approximately the chin.

Design Technique

Hair is dried and then set on hot sticks in a spiral fashion from roots to ends. This creates the soft curl look. Spray each strand with a sculpting spray before setting.

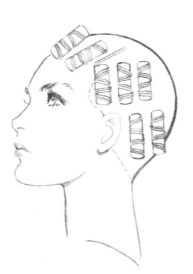

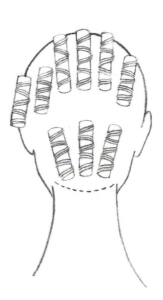

Styling Technique

Do not brush the hair as this will relax the curl. Simply use a wide tooth comb or pick and separate the curls. Direct light side back and up. Hold with a finishing spray. Lift top bang area up and back, and again, hold with a finishing spray. To insure longer lasting curls, spray with finishing spray. Using a blower set on low speed and cool air, move blower in a circular pattern directing air up into the curls for a few seconds.

Style

4

Cutting Technique

All hair is held straight down using horizontal partings and cut parallel to the floor with the head held straight. Length from nape hairline should be about 4½ inches. Finished cut should have a very slight graduation.

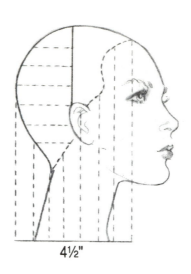

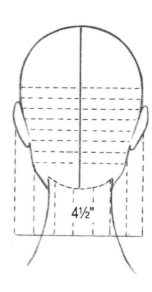

4½"

4½"

1. On Base
2. 1/2 Base
3. Off Base

Design Technique

Hair should be set on base with a side part with medium rollers across the top of the head and down heavy side. Light side should be set off base. Top is rolled straight back on base and the back is rolled down. A blow dryer and hot rollers can also be used successfully to create the softness of this style.

Note: Use smaller rollers on fine hair and larger on course hair.

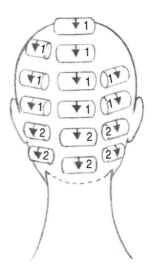

Styling Technique

Hair should be brushed with a styling brush. Brush back away from the face. Brush in waves around face then fluff the ends with pick to create curls at ends. This style can be backcombed for more height and fullness or simply brushed into shape.

Style

5

Cutting Technique

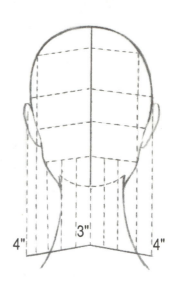

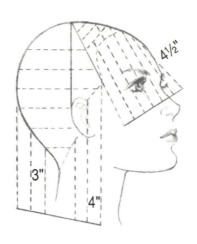

Back of hair is cut with head looking down to create an undercut. Back should be cut to a 3 inch at center of the nape in a slight V shape to accent increasing length towards front. Sides are cut with the head leaned over to the opposite shoulder, again to create an undercut. Be sure not to elevate sides or back. Then bangs are cut from a horseshoe section 2 inches deep between recession points. Cut a diagonal line starting at the center of the eye on the left side and finishing at midear on the right side. Graduate slightly with each parting.

Design Technique

Back and sides are blown dry under, using a round brush. Be sure to remove 80 percent of the moisture before using the round brush. Using sections the size of the diameter of the brush, overdirect hair and dry from roots to ends. This will increase fullness and direct moisture to the ends of hair. Direct air toward ends when almost dry. Allow to cool and remove brush. Dry bang across front using diagonal partings. Additional curl may be added by using a 1 inch curling iron around the perimeter. Make sure to make only one complete circle with the iron.

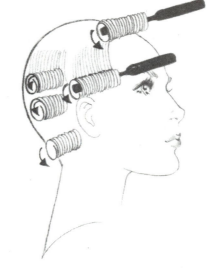

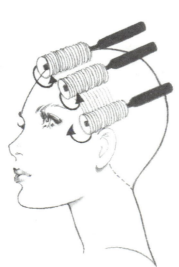

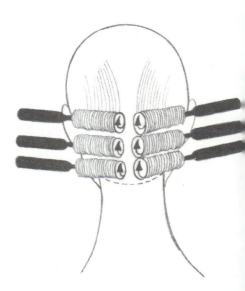

Styling Technique

Brush through hair ends encouraging hair to turn under. Brush under strand and on top of strand using free hand to guide hair on brush. Brush across bang section to create movement.

Style

6

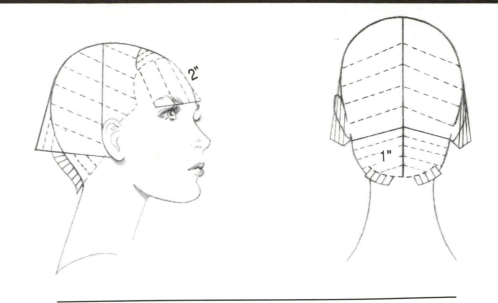

Cutting Technique

Section the nape from the occipital bone to the center of the ear. This will create a diamond-shaped section. Cut this entire section at high elevation to 1 inch. Cut the crown on a diagonal following the line created by the nape section. Hold at low elevation and cut. The sides will be cut at the same diagonal line as the back causing an increase of length towards the face. Using a horseshoe section in the bang approximately 2 inches deep, cut the bangs to the bridge of the nose. Then texturize the bang area for height.

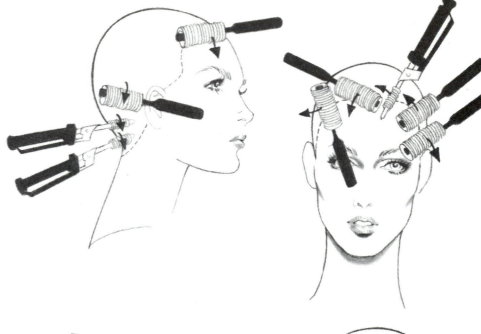

Design Technique

This style will be blown dry close to the head with the exception of the bangs which will have height. Remove 80 percent of the moisture from the hair before using the brush. Using a round brush, dry the hair from roots to ends. Be sure to work from the bottom up. Wrap the hair around the brush and dry on the top and bottom. Allow to cool, then remove brush. This will strengthen the set. In bang area, use a small diameter round brush. Over-direct the hair around the brush and dry. A large barrel curling iron can be used on the ends and bangs. Follow the same pattern. Do not turn iron around the hair more than once except in the bangs which should be set on base.

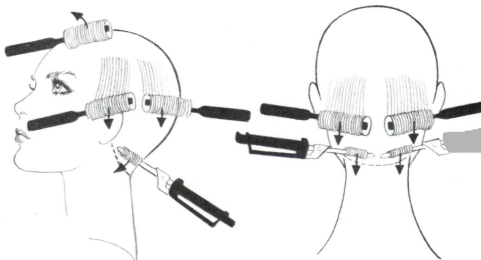

Styling Technique

Smooth all the hair under around the weight line. Bang area should be lifted up away from the head. Use a light back-combing and or spray if needed.

7

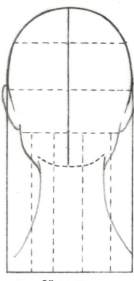

8"

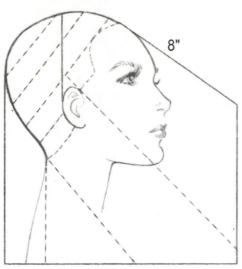

8" or more

8" or more

Cutting Technique

Section hair into four sections dividing the back in half from the top of the crown to the nape and the front down the center. Cut all the hair in back horizontal to the floor at a low elevation with the head in an upright position. The sides are cut by holding the hand at a 45 degree angle at the center of the face starting at the tip of the nose and then cutting vertically down. Make sure to direct the hair forward in front of the face.

Design Technique

This style will be done on dry hair. Block head into 14 sections, 5 across the front and 9 across the back. Take one section at a time and spray lightly with a sculpting spray. Twist until the hair spins around itself. Wrap the end around the knot and secure with a bobbie pin. When all the sections are completed, place head under a dryer for 30 minutes.

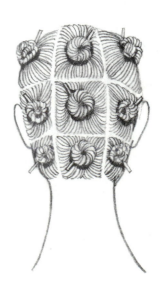

Styling Technique

Allow hair to cool, then gently unwind each curl. Using a wide-tooth comb, gently separate and blend together all the sections. Do not over comb, this will relax the set. The finished style will have deep waves and a wild fun look. Spray with a light holding spray.

Note: Each section will be approximately 2 inches by 3 inches.

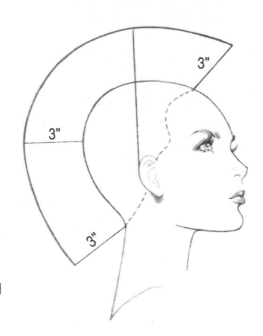

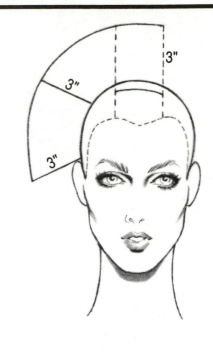

Cutting Technique

The cut is an equal blend with each hair measuring 3 inches. Be sure to hold the hair straight out from the head at a 90 degree angle and cut the hair parallel to the head form. This will create a rounded look. The hair can be lightly texturized if the style is to be backcombed.

1. On Base
2. 1/2 Base
3. Off Base

Design Technique

Set the top of the head rolling the hair diagonally back from the right of center all the way to the left side of the nape. The hair should go around the roller 1½ turns. Take a triangular section at the hairline and place a roller directed forward. This roller will be perpendicular to the diagonal line of the rollers. To create an upward movement on the sides, comb the hair upward, then around a roller directed back and diagonally down. Rollers on the right side of the top diagonal line will pivot into the center of the back. Rollers on the right side will pivot to fill the right nape area.

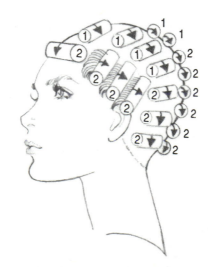

Styling Technique

Hair should be brushed to relax the set. Follow the lines of the setting pattern and direct the hair. Sides should be brushed up and back to enhance the up and back movement. The bang will form a wave that will dip down over the left side of the forehead. To create a fuller smoother look, backcomb and smooth only the ends following the direction of the set.

9

Cutting Technique

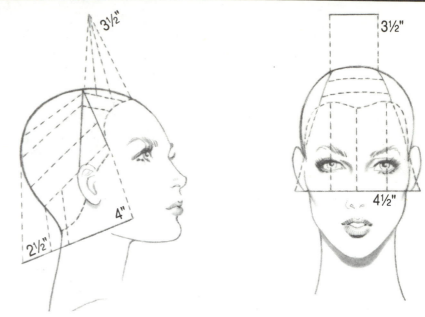

The bang section will be cut to end of the nose. Then cut a guide 3½ inches at top of the crown. Comb hair back to the stationary guide and cut all that does not reach. This will increase length to the front. Back is cut rounded towards the front blending into the sides and creating a diagonal upward line from back to front. Back and sides should be under cut to encourage hair to bend under.

Design Technique

Back is dried under and straight down. Sides are dried down on a diagonal line. Be sure to direct root area up to create fullness. Bangs are dried around a small round brush moving across the head from the part. First section should be dried on base, second half base, and third off base to allow bangs to fall over the eye. On ebony hair, a curling iron will be needed to reinforce and smooth the hair. A large barrel (1") should be used around the perimeter, and a medium barrel (¾") on the bangs.

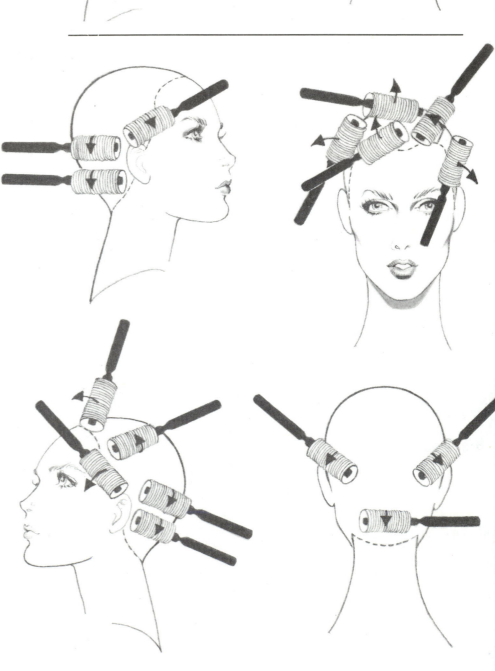

Styling Technique

Simply comb hair down and under around the perimeter. Bang area will be brushed back diagonally and then pushed forward over one eye. Pull hair down with thumb and forefinger over one eye and use your other hand to hold wave. On Caucasian hair, some light back combing might be needed.

Style

10

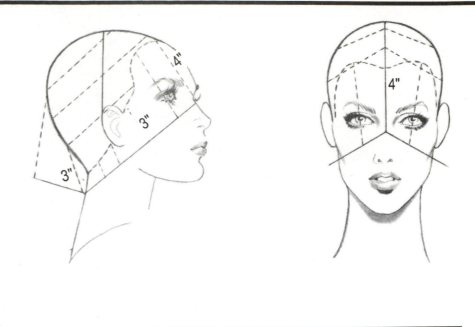

Cutting Technique

This is a low elevation cut which is very slightly graduated in the back. The graduation will allow the hair to stack. To cut the back, keep head in an upright position. This combined with slight tension will create the needed graduation. Then cut using diagonal partings a line from the bridge of the nose to the longest length in the back.

Design Technique

Hair is blown dry using a wide-tooth comb. Comb hair straight out from the head with dryer following the comb. This will help to smooth and straighten the hair. After drying, use a large barrel curling iron on 1 inch thick partings and smooth hair over the iron from roots to ends. Smooth each parting curl ends one revolution around iron. In the bang area using the same iron, set two curls on base, one curl half base, and one curl off base to create the height and movement.

Note: This style should be done on chemically relaxed hair.

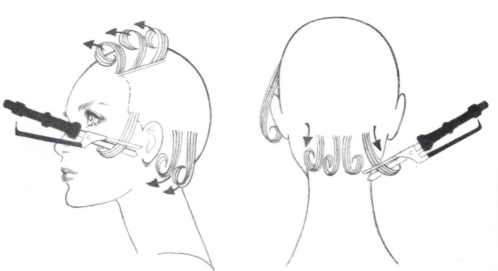

Styling Technique

Spray hair with a light finishing oil and comb through. Hair is simply smoothed with a comb and turned under at the ends in the back and on the sides. The bang area is combed up away from the head. Tuck ends under. A holding spray will be needed to maintain height in front.

Style

11

Cutting Technique

Using horizontal partings, cut back parallel to floor with head looking down. Sides should be cut parallel to floor with head tilted to side to create a natural undercut. Bang section will be taken from center low point on natural recession to high point of crown. Cut all hair in this section to 3½ inches. Texturize lightly with razor or texturizing shear.

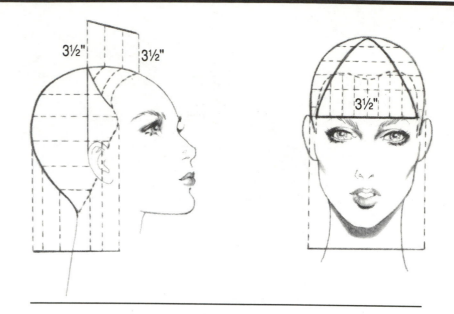

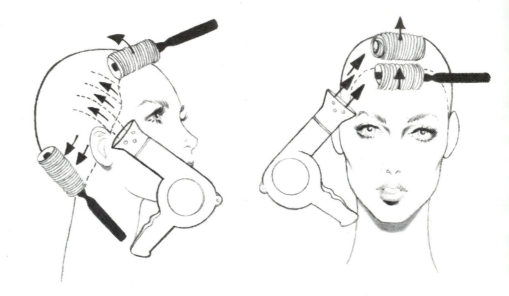

Design Technique

Hair is air waved. Starting in the back, dry by overdirecting hair up for fullness. Dry from roots to ends, then just before the hair is completely dry, roll hair around a round brush. Direct blower on both sides of brush to set curl. Let cool and remove. Using a sculpting spray, direct hair on sides up and slightly back. Leave ends slightly damp and dry curl into ends. Top should be directed back around a medium round brush.

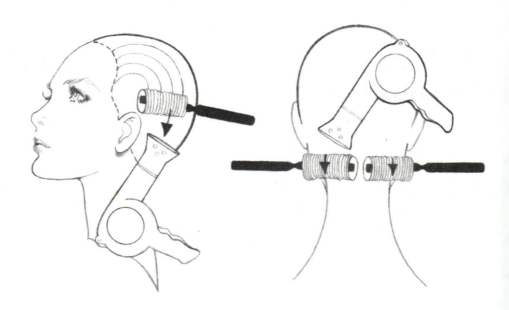

Styling Technique

Top will need to be back brushed or lightly back combed for support and height. Back brush sides up and away from the face for support and fullness. Spray with a firm finishing spray. Back is blended into the sides by lacing the sides (lightly back combing or brushing the ends) into the back.

Style

12

Cutting Technique

Hair is cut to a hanging length of 6 inches. Holding head in upright position, cut all hair horizontal to floor using tension to create graduated ends. Proceed to lightly texturize ends using a texturizing shear or razor removing about 20 percent of the bulk. Cut bangs using a horseshoe section 3 inches deep and to the center of the recession on either side.

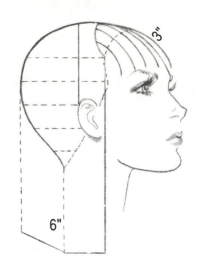

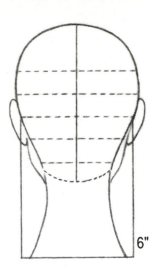

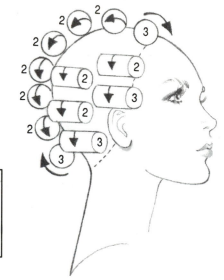

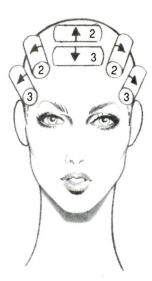

1.	On Base
2.	1/2 Base
3.	Off Base

Design Technique

Use two large rollers directed down on the sides and set on base. Back will be set down using large rollers with the exception of the bottom roller which will be turned up. The bang is set forward and off base.

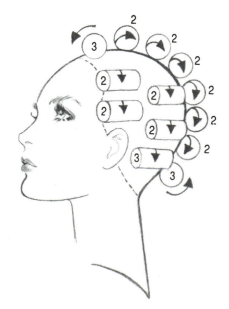

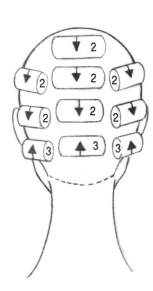

24

Styling Technique

Using a styling brush, brush hair flat to head and break down set. Then starting in center of the back brush hair flat to the head, and then at the end of the strand lift hair up and away to create the flip. Work towards the front completing one side at a time. Brush bangs down and out to sides.

Style

13

Cutting Technique

Cut hair in standard one length bob. Hold head straight and cut parallel to floor. Use tension and head position to create a slight graduation at ends. Remove excess bulk with a texturizing shear or razor to allow waves to hold in the styling.

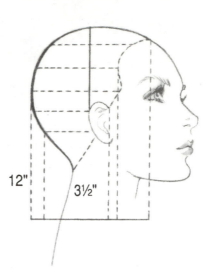

12"   3½"

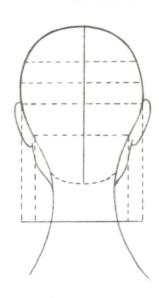

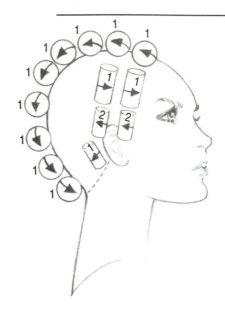

1. On Base
2. 1/2 Base
3. Off Base

Design Technique

Top is set on rollers straight back and on base for fullness all the way to the nape. Sides are set vertically with the top row rolled towards the face on base and the second row set towards the back. By alternating direction of rollers, we increase the intensity of the waves. These two rows will continue to the center row in the back. The nape is set diagonally down towards the center.

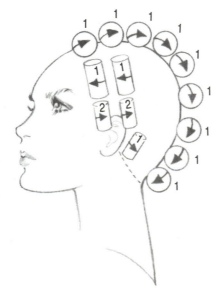

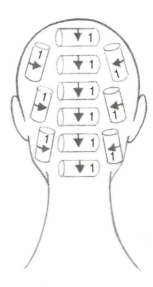

Styling Technique

Brush hair to break down set and develop waves. Back comb entire set building a base only on top. Sides should be lightly back combed. Starting on top, direct hair with a brush into the wave pattern. Use fingers of free hand to hold waves in place. Procedure for holding waves is similar to finger waving. Use less pressure to hold hair. Work horizontally down sides lightly brushing waves into place.

14

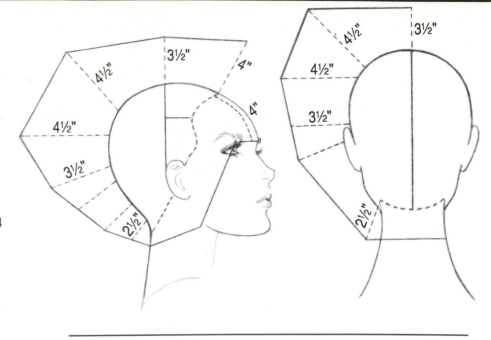

Cutting Technique

This cut is a blended layer cut starting at 4 inches in the bangs and increasing to a maximum length of 4½ inches at the occipital. This cut must be texturized heavily on the ends (approximately the last 2½") with a razor or by slide cutting so that the ends appear wispy. This will also help develop the full form.

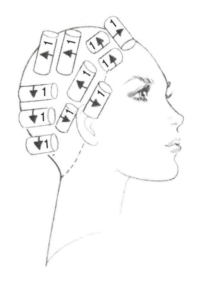

1.	On Base
2.	1/2 Base
3.	Off Base

Design Technique

Starting in the nape, blow dry hair diagonally down and forward. Crown is dried down in the center, then the rest diagonally towards the center. Be sure to overdirect hair throughout the style so as to create a full look. Sides are over-directed back and rolled around the brush towards the face. The top is dried in two directions. The right center is dried straight back and the left center is directed across the head. For styles on ebony-hair finish, follow the same pattern with a large (1") curling iron.

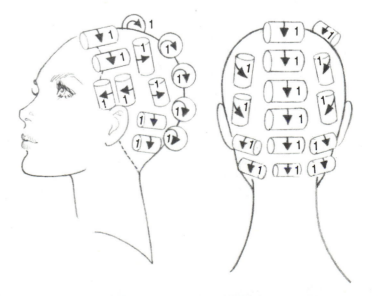

Styling Technique

Using a styling pick, flick hair up and out. Separate ends using finger tips or pick. Pull bang area down over left eye. Be sure to use a light touch so as not to make ends appear heavy.

Note: Ebony hair should not need backcombing. If this style is on a mannequin or Caucasian, light backcombing might be needed.

Style

15

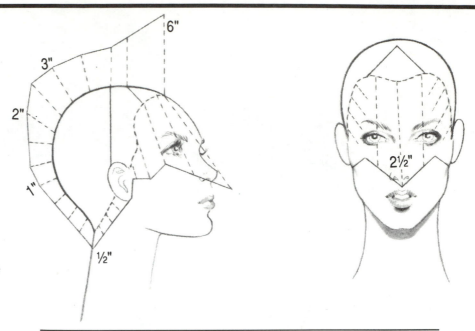

Cutting Technique

Cut the back using a high elevation starting in the nape at ½ inch. Work up to the top of the crown which is 3 inches. Cut the sides starting at 2 up to 3-inch length on top. The bang section is a triangle approximately 2½ inches deep. This will be the last section cut. Blend the top into the bang. Use a slide cut technique, shear blades open but not moving, to maintain 6-inch length in the bang. Be sure to blend the perimeter length in the bang to the perimeter in the temporals. Again, a slide cut method is recommended.

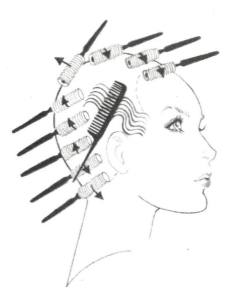

Design Technique

Dry the nape area first using a blower. Direct blower and nape hair down. The center of the crown will be dried diagonally up. The sides are air waved using the blower and comb. Comb hair up at the hairline, then create a ridge by pushing the comb down and forward, like finger waving. Direct the blower on a low setting through the comb. When the ridge is dried, move back 1 inch, then direct a second ridge up and forward. Repeat the process on the other side. The top should be dried forward using the fingers or a small round brush. Use a mousse or light gel to develop height and separation.

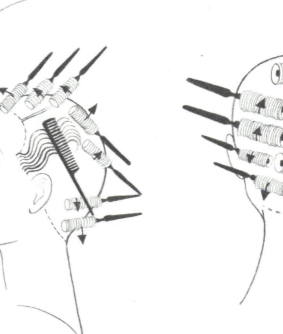

Styling Technique

Brush the sides back. Use a good holding spray. Lift top and bangs with fingers or styling pick and spray with a firm hold spray. To increase separation, use a blower on low while spraying.

Style
16

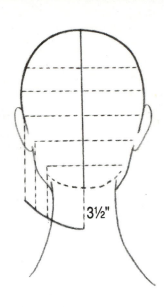

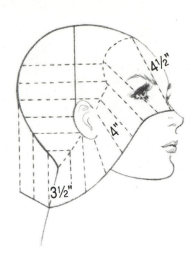

Cutting Technique

Layers are cut around the face by over-directing the hair to the perimeter line. This will create softness around the face. The back is cut in a stack by holding the head upright, using tension, and a slight elevation. Cut the back in a soft arc to create rounded shape.

Design Technique

Finger wave the top starting 2 inches from the part and directing the ridge forward. Make a second ridge back to the top of the crown. On the light side create a ridge towards the face. Stop at the crown. Complete the head with alternating rows of pincurls.

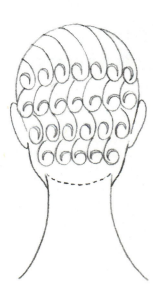

Styling Technique

Brush the hair to soften the set. Then reinforce the fingerwaves by holding with
fingers and spraying with a holding spray.
Next, using a lift, separate the pincurls
and pull hair away from head to create
the casual look.

Style
17

Cutting Technique

Hair is cut in a basic bob approximately 1 inch longer than center of hairline in the nape. Use approximately 1 inch partings throughout cut. All remaining hair is combed down and cut straight across using tension. Place head down when cutting first two partings creating an undercut. The rest of back will be cut with head held straight. Cut sides with a very slight diagonal shorter to the front using the mouth as a guide. Keep head in an upright position throughout. Then, cut interior in a reverse elevation to a length of 5 inches. All hair should be brought straight up to guide.

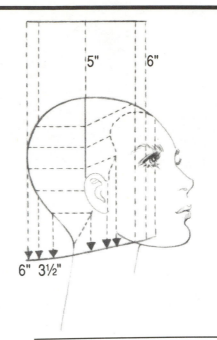

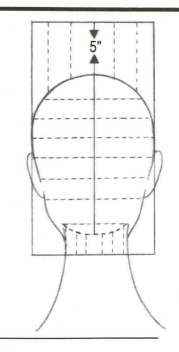

1. On Base
2. 1/2 Base
3. Off Base

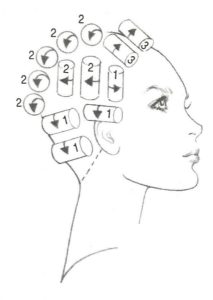

Design Technique

Style can be blown dry or set on rollers and then thermal curled. Using a medium size roller or a ¾ curling iron, set top from side part off base. One roller on light side is set forward, the rest back. Heavy side has two rollers set forward. The rest of rollers on sides are directed back to center of crown. Rest of back is set down.

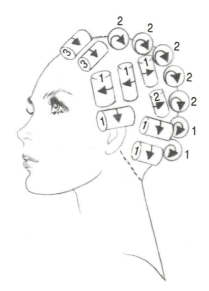

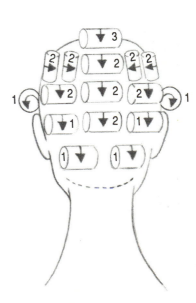

Styling Technique

The style gives the feel of natural curl, therefore, do not over brush or comb. If using curling iron, use a wide tooth comb to separate curls. If using rollers, brush hair just enough to soften the set. Direct hair away from the face using wide tooth comb and then push forward. Use a small amount of styling gel or mousse on combed hair to separate curl, then finish with a light holding spray.

Style

18

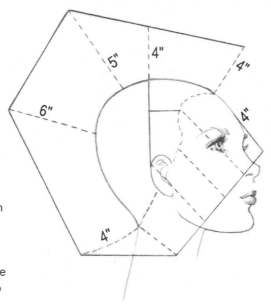
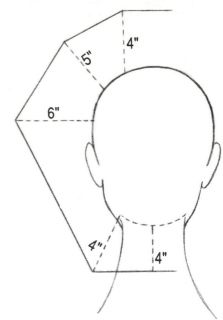

Cutting Technique

This is a layered style using high elevation and overdirection to create length in the crown and nape. Perimeter is cut to a 4-inch length around the head. Interior is cut from 4 inches on top to 6 inches at the center of the crown. Blend all lengths into the perimeter.

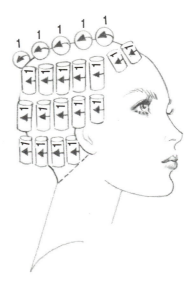

1. On Base
2. 1/2 Base
3. Off Base

Design Technique

One row of filler rollers are set across the bang area to create movement. The top is set straight back. The rest of the rollers are set vertically to the center of the back. To create curl, be sure the winds around the rollers are 2½ times.

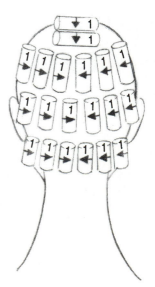

Styling Technique

Do not brush the hair. Use a comb and gently comb through each curl. Then lightly backcomb each curl to develop height and to stretch out each curl. After backcombing each curl, use a metal lift or end of a tail comb to lift last inch hair out and reform curls. Hair should have a naturally curly look.

19

Cutting Technique

The cut is longer on top starting at 3½ inches and tapers down to 2 inches over the ears and 1 inch at the nape. Be sure to square the top. The form is a diamond, so do not cut rounded shapes. Do this by cutting straight lines and holding hands constant throughout center top, then rounded sides then flat sides.

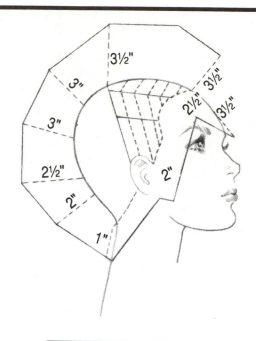

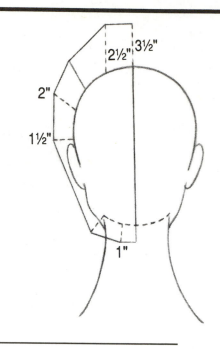

1. On Base
2. 1/2 Base
3. Off Base

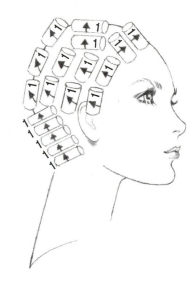

Design Technique

Hair should be dried up and away from the face throughout the head. Bang area should be dried up and into the center. Using a mini barrel (¼") curling iron, curl all hair from roots to ends, diagonally up, and towards the center. This will create a full form. Top rollers should oppose each other creating a casual curly look.

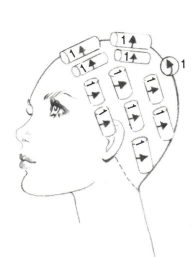

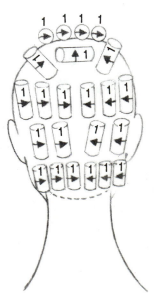

Styling Technique

Simply pick out the curl and direct back. Bangs should be pulled down over the middle of the forehead. Lightly pat curl back into the diamond shape after picking. Be sure not to brush or over work the hair. This will relax the curl.

Style

20

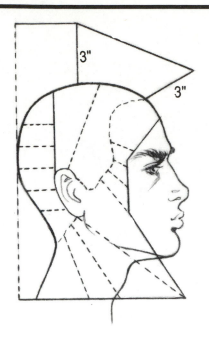

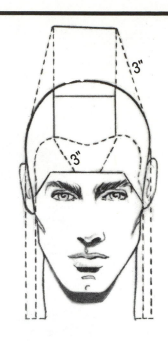

Cutting Technique

Cut the entire perimeter horizontal to the floor. Then cut the bang section to the top of the eyebrows (3"). Temporal area is cut to 2 inches directing the hair forward towards the eyes. Blend temporal areas with back and bang. Cut top section to 3 inches from the bang to top of the crown. Be sure to cut 3-inch length to the temporal area. Blend the rest of the hair by pulling up to the top. Cut only the hair that reaches.

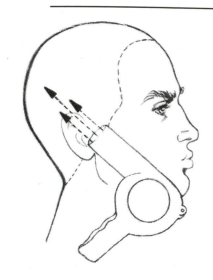

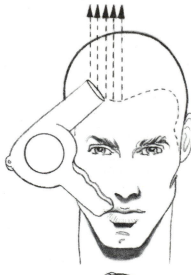

Design Technique

Dry top with blower directing hair straight back. Sides are dried directing the hair diagonally up and back. Dry back using a diffuser to avoid disturbing curl.

Note: This style should be done on naturally curly hair or permed hair.

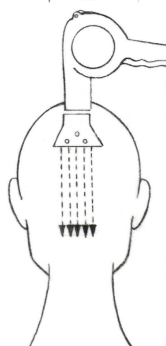

Styling Technique

Brush sides and top back using a vent brush or wide tooth comb. Do not brush the back as this will create excessive volume. Spray with a light hold finishing spray.

Style 21

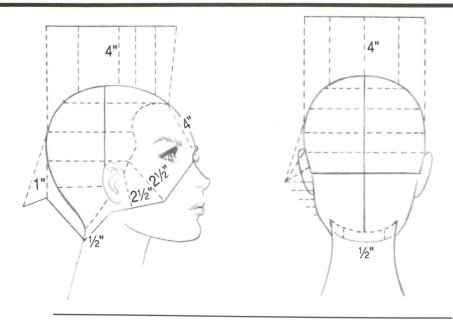

Cutting Technique

Section horizontally from the top of the ear to the top of the other ear. All hair in the lower section will be cut at a high elevation starting at ½ inch at the hairline to 2 inches at top of section. Bring the rest of the hair down to the lower section and cut at a low elevation. To add softness, layer by pulling all hair straight up and cutting to a 5 inch length at top of the crown. Only a small portion of the hair will reach the guide.

Design Technique

Hair is styled across the top on a bias. Air wave with a large round brush directing the back down and under. Sides should be dried diagonally back and down. The heavy side of the top should be dried forward and the light side across.

Styling Technique

Brush hair on sides up and back using a vent brush. For more volume, spray with a light holding spray while brushing. On top, use fingers and shake through the hair to create separation and texture. Pull small amounts of hair straight down in bang area. Use a light holding spray to keep hair separated.

22

Cutting Technique

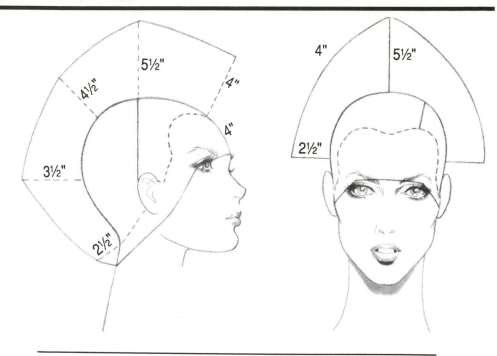

Cut the perimeter in the nape to a length of 2½ inches. Following the hairline, cut of the perimeter at 2½ inches through the sides. Cut the bangs to the bridge of the nose (4"). Proceed to blend the sides into the bangs. Cut the interior from 2½ inches in the nape to 5½ inches at the top of the crown. Blend top of the crown into a 4-inch bang length, then blend sides from 2½ to 5½ inches at top.

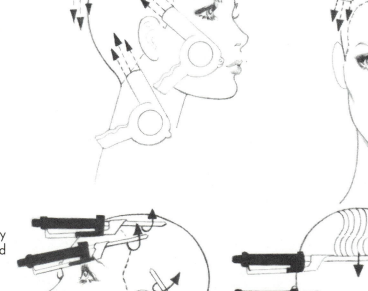

Design Technique

Starting in the back, dry hair up and away from the head. The crown should be dried under and diagonally towards the heavy side. The lower 2 inches of the sides should be dried up the same as the back and the rest of the sides and top dried down and under. Dry a 1-inch section of the bangs forward and under and the rest across. Style can then be reinforced using a 1-inch barrel curling iron following the same pattern.

Styling Technique

This is a casual style that is brushed with a vent brush or directed with the fingers. The sides are brushed up and back. Then move the rest of the hair in a circular pattern starting in the bang section and moving to the back. A light hold finishing spray can be used to hold the set.

23

Cutting Technique

Cut a soft taper from the nape to the occipital. Simply take a 2-inch parting and overdirect to top of parting throughout the nape. This procedure will be repeated throughout hairline except in the bang section. At occipital, decrease elevation throughout crown to increase length. Hair should be approximately 4 inches at top of crown. Sides are cut using the crown and the perimeter cut as a guide. Longest hanging length on side should be 4 inches. Bangs are cut to 4 inches and blended into the sides. Hair is then cut in a reverse elevation with a crown length of 3½ inches. All hair is brought up to guide on top. Razor or tapering shears should be used to create texture throughout cut.

Design Technique

Hair is blown dry with a forward direction. Work mousse or light styling lotion through hair. A large round brush or hands should be used to create movement. Overdirect hair in crown and top areas. Start in bang section and work towards back.

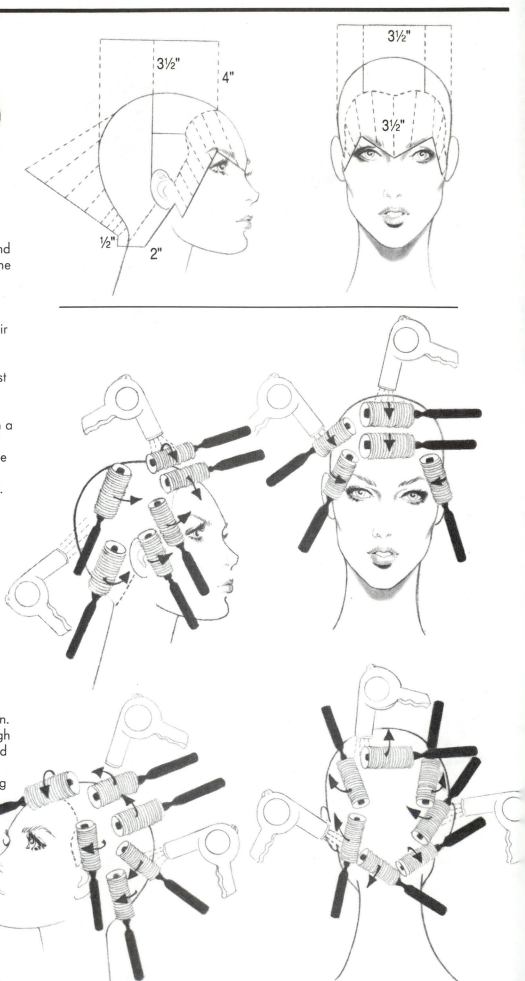

Styling Technique

Tousle hair with hands pushing hair towards the face to create a casual look. Use a light sculpting spray or mousse on the ends to create separation and texture in hair.

Style
24

Cutting Technique

This cut is a high elevation with top and sides cut to 3½ inches and the back tapered down to approximately 1½ inches. As with all short cuts, the nape can be adjusted to clients growth patterns.

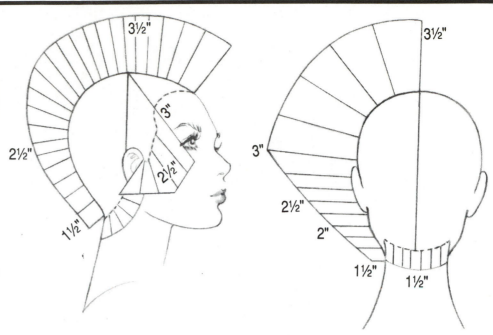

Design Technique

Hair is blown dry with round brushes. Start in nape drying under and down. Sides and crown are dried diagonally up, towards the center, and overdirected for fullness. Top is dried back and bangs are directed across and down. A ¾-inch curling iron can be used to reinforce the style.

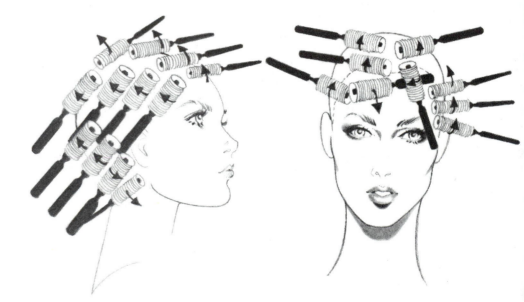

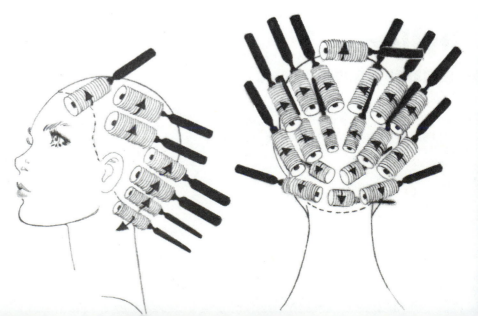

Styling Technique

Use a vent brush to comb hair diagonally back and up. Pull a small amount of hair down over the forehead in bang area to create softness. Nape should be turned under. Top can be lightly backbrushed for more fullness.

Style

25

Cutting Technique

Back of head is cut horizontal to the floor. Sides are angled up towards the face. Then a line is cut from the bridge of the nose down to the side length. Hair is then cut in a reverse elevation using a diagonal line from 6 inches at the back of the crown to 4 inches at the bang. Then proceed to heavily texturize, removing at least 30 percent of the hair starting 2 inches from the scalp to the ends.

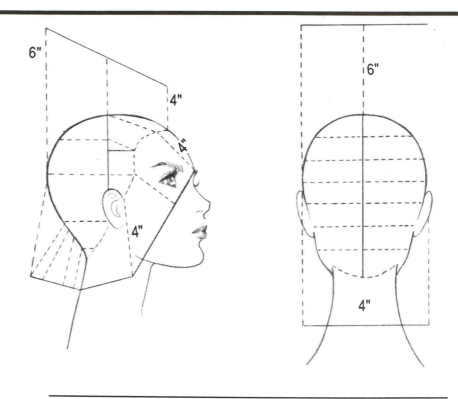

Design Technique

Blow dry this style by scrunching, using the palm of the hand in a circular motion flat to the head. This creates the uneven tousled look. In the bang area, create direction by twisting and drying hair in desired direction. On the sides of the face, direct hair up and away from head.

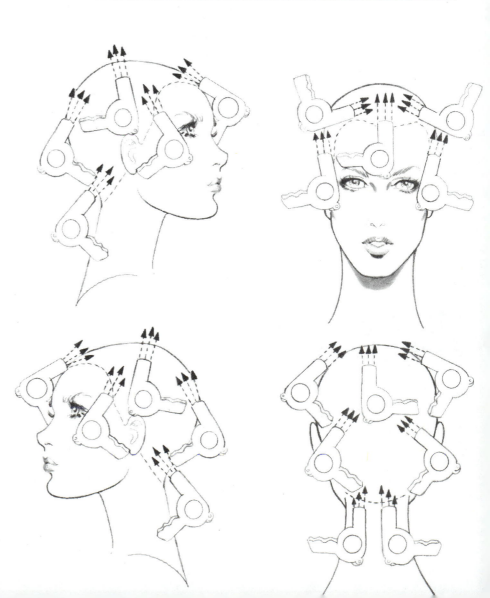

Styling Technique

This is a casual style that cannot be exactly duplicated. When dry, use fingertips or metal prong pick to lift ends out away from head. Do not brush the hair as this will smooth the style. Direct bangs and sides using fingers. Be sure not to over work the hair.

Style

26

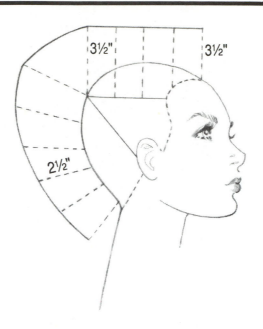

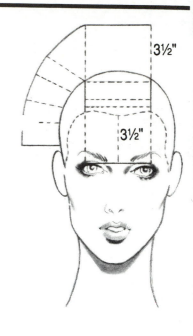

Cutting Technique

Cut the hair to 3½ inches equal blend throughout top. Sides and back are blended in at 2½ inches. This is an ideal length for fingerwaving ebony hair.

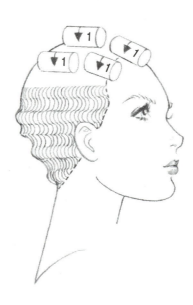

1. On Base
2. 1/2 Base
3. Off Base

Design Technique

Section off a horizontal line around the head from the low point of the recession. Clip top out of the way. Using a heavy gel, work throughout the sides and back. Fingerwaves can be set using either the traditional method or the pencil wave method. Once you have mastered the horizontal pattern, try diagonal and vertical pattern waves. Top can be either set or curled with an iron. If using the iron, be sure to comb hair across from the part, then dry under hooded dryer. Set all curls across the top of the head.

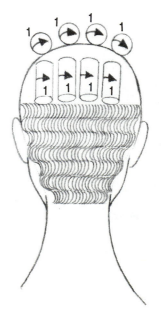

Styling Technique

Do NOT brush the fingerwaves. Simply spray with a strong holding hair spray. Top can be picked for a casual look or brushed into waves for a more sophisticated look.

27

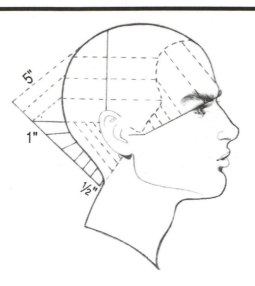

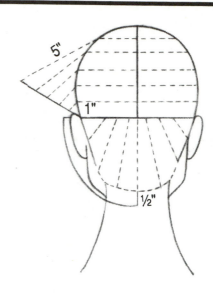

Cutting Technique

Create a horseshoe section in the nape from the top of the left ear to the top of the right ear. Nape is cut from ½ inch at hairline to 1 inch at the part line. Using low elevation, cut remaining hair in crown from 1 inch, using nape section as a guide, to maximum of 5 inches. On the heavy side, using the crown as a guide, cut at low elevation from 1 to 5-inch length. On the light side, the cut will be from 1 to 3 inches. Bangs will be cut to the bridge of the nose and blended into the sides.

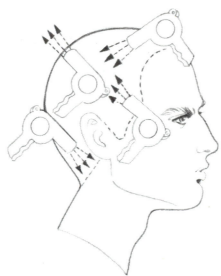

Design Technique

Starting in the back, dry down in the nape area. Crown should be dried diagonally towards the center and up. Proceed to side and direct straight back. Heavy side of top should be directed back at the part and then across the top. At the weight line, direct ends of hair up for accent.

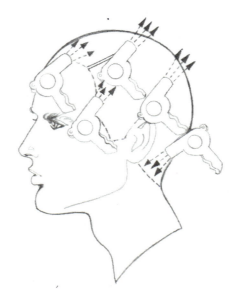

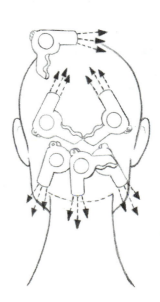

Styling Technique

Brush all hair back from the front to back. Insert the teeth of a vent brush into the weight line and pull hair back and up to accent the line.

28

Cutting Technique

Nape guide should be established to 3 inches. The perimeter around the front hairline should be cut 1 inch up to temple. Bangs should be 4 inches and cut to meet sides. Perimeter over the ear should be mid ear. The layers are squared off through the top and sides to create a square silhouette. Back is slightly over-directed to create fullness. Clean out area from sideburn to the ear. This area does not have to blend with hair over ear.

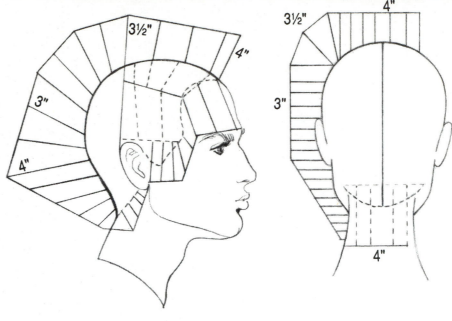

Design Technique

Hair should be styled using a mousse or sculpting lotion. Using blow dry and fingers, direct sides back close to head. On top, overdirect hair back for fullness. Bang is dried across front with ½ bang section dried in forward direction and overdirected on base. Back is directed diagonally downward to create movement without fullness.

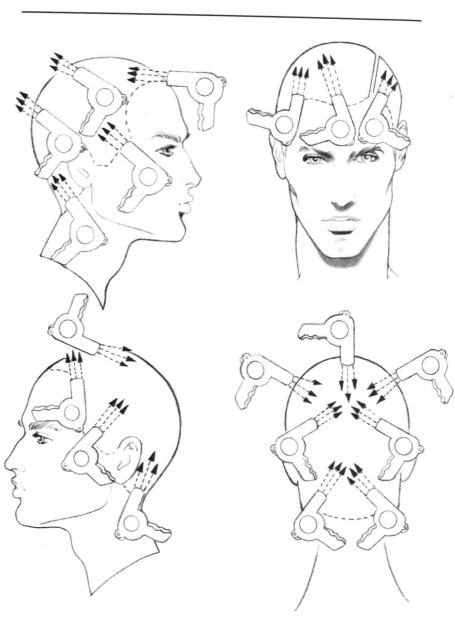

Styling Technique

Hair should be left casual. Do not over comb or attempt to smooth style. After drying, tousle hair with fingers to create a wind blown look.

TERMINOLOGY LIST

ANGLE: Position in which hair is held away from the headform to create elevation in haircutting. Degree of elevation used to determine roller relation to base in setting.

BACKBRUSH: Brushing the hair toward the scalp while holding the ends of the hair strands up and out from the head.

BACKCOMB: Combing small sections of hair from the ends toward the scalp, causing the shorter hair to mat at scalp, forming a cushion or base; tease.

BASE: Portion of a curl attached to the scalp.

BEVELCUT: Haircut with an oblique line at edge of strand, similar to bevel edge of a mirror.

BEVELCUTTING: Haircutting technique of rolling the strand upward before cutting so that top of strand is very slightly shorter, encouraging hair to turn upward. See illustration. (See also **undercutting** for alternate technique.)

BLEND: To mix or mingle together, so that the line of demarcation cannot be distinguished.

CANDLESTICK: Setting pattern in which rollers are placed vertically.

CARVED CURL: A pin curl sliced from a shaping and formed without lifting the hair from the head.

CLOCKWISE: Movement in the same direction as the hands of a clock.

CONTROL BRUSHING: Comb-out technique to relax setting pattern where hair is brushed with one hand and followed through the palm of the other hand to mold hair into design line.

DESIGN LINE: Artistic concept of finished style as expressed in lines and shapes.

DIAMETER: Distance across a roller or pin curl through the center.

ELEVATION: The angle or degree hair is held from the headform. No elevation—hair is held flat against headform to create length. Low—hair is held 15 degrees up from the headform. Medium—45 degrees. High—90 degrees. See illustration.

ELONGATED: Extended, lengthened, stretched out.

GRADUATE: Another term for layering. Cutting the hair with elevation so that each subsequent subsection is shorter than the guide.

GUIDELINE: Section of hair at the nape or at sides of head cut to a specified length. This "line" provides the measuring device for cutting the rest of the hair.

HEIGHT: Volume from the top of the headform to create illusion of length.

HORIZONTAL: Parallel to the horizon; level.

INDENTATION: Curved hollow or valley created in the formation of a hairstyle.

LAYERS: Graduated effect achieved by cutting the hair with elevation so that each subsequent subsection is slightly shorter than the guide.

OBLIQUE: Neither vertical nor horizontal; slanted, inclined.

OBLONG: An elongated oval shape.

OFF BASE: Strand is held at 70 degrees so that curl is placed off its base.

½ OFF BASE: Strand is held at 90 degrees so that curl is placed one-half off its base.

ON BASE: Strand is held at 125 degrees so that curl is placed in the center of its base.

PIE-SHAPED: Triangular or wedge-shaped.

PIVOT: The exact point from which the hair is directed in forming a curvature or shaping.

RIBBON: Hair setting technique in which hair is forced between thumb and back of comb to create tension. Gives control to set and body to comb-out.

RIDGE: Crest of a wave.

SECTION: Divide the hair by parting into separate areas for control.

SHAPING: The formation of uniform arcs or curves in wet hair, providing a base for finger waves, pin curls, or various patterns in hairstyling.

STAND-UP CURL: A curl with the stem directed straight up or out from the head and clipped in a standing position.

STEM: Part of a curl between the base and the first arc of the circle.

SUBSECTION: Further division of the section into exact strands to be cut. Amount for each subsection varies with texture and density of hair as well as cutting technique.

SURFACE COMB: Comb-out technique of lightly smoothing style with hairstyling comb to refine design lines.

TAPER: Shorten the hair in a graduated effect.

TEASE: Another term for backcomb.

TENSION: Stress caused by stretching or pulling.

UNDERCUTTING: Haircutting technique of reverse elevation in which each subsection is cut slightly longer than the guide to encourage hair to turn under. See illustration.

VERTICAL: In an upright position. Perpendicular to the horizon.

VOLUME: Mass or fullness beyond the shape of the head.

Grading Record

Note: Each time a style is performed, your instructor will grade it on a scale of 1-10. A grade of 5 to 6 is average, and any grade below that shows a serious need for improvement.

STYLE 1

Date	Grade	Instructor	Instructor's Comments

STYLE 2

Date	Grade	Instructor	Instructor's Comments

STYLE 3

Date	Grade	Instructor	Instructor's Comments

STYLE 4

Date	Grade	Instructor	Instructor's Comments

STYLE 5

Date	Grade	Instructor	Instructor's Comments

STYLE 6

Date	Grade	Instructor	Instructor's Comments

STYLE 7

Date	Grade	Instructor	Instructor's Comments

STYLE 8

Date	Grade	Instructor	Instructor's Comments

STYLE 9

Date	Grade	Instructor	Instructor's Comments

STYLE 10

Date	Grade	Instructor	Instructor's Comments

STYLE 11

Date	Grade	Instructor	Instructor's Comments

STYLE 12

Date	Grade	Instructor	Instructor's Comments

STYLE 13

Date	Grade	Instructor	Instructor's Comments

STYLE 14

Date	Grade	Instructor	Instructor's Comments

STYLE 15

Date	Grade	Instructor	Instructor's Comments

STYLE 16

Date	Grade	Instructor	Instructor's Comments

STYLE 17

Date	Grade	Instructor	Instructor's Comments

STYLE 18

Date	Grade	Instructor	Instructor's Comments

STYLE 19

Date	Grade	Instructor	Instructor's Comments

STYLE 20

Date	Grade	Instructor	Instructor's Comments

STYLE 21

Date	Grade	Instructor	Instructor's Comments

STYLE 22

Date	Grade	Instructor	Instructor's Comments

STYLE 23

Date	Grade	Instructor	Instructor's Comments

STYLE 24

Date	Grade	Instructor	Instructor's Comments

STYLE 25

Date	Grade	Instructor	Instructor's Comments

STYLE 26

Date	Grade	Instructor	Instructor's Comments

STYLE 27

Date	Grade	Instructor	Instructor's Comments

STYLE 28

Date	Grade	Instructor	Instructor's Comments